The Complete Poems
of
The Earl of Rochester

John Wilmot, the Earl of Rochester

Filiquarian Publishing, LLC

Contents

A Fragment of Seneca Translated

After Death nothing is, and nothing, death,
The utmost limit of a gasp of breath.
Let the ambitious zealot lay aside
His hopes of heaven, whose faith is but his pride;
Let slavish souls lay by their fear
Nor be concerned which way nor where
After this life they shall be hurled.
Dead, we become the lumber of the world,
And to that mass of matter shall be swept
Where things destroyed with things unborn are kept.
Devouring time swallows us whole.
Impartial death confounds body and soul.
For Hell and the foul fiend that rules
God's everlasting fiery jails
(Devised by rogues, dreaded by fools),
With his grim, grisly dog that keeps the door,
Are senseless stories, idle tales,
Dreams, whimsey's, and no more.

John Wilmot, the Earl of Rochester

A Letter from Artemesia in the Town to Chloe in the Country

Chloe,

In verse by your command I write.
Shortly you'll bid me ride astride, and fight:
These talents better with our sex agree
Than lofty flights of dangerous poetry.
Amongst the men, I mean the men of wit
(At least they passed for such before they writ),
How many bold adventureers for the bays,
Proudly designing large returns of praise,
Who durst that stormy, pathless world explore,
Were soon dashed back, and wrecked on the dull shore,
Broke of that little stock they had before!
How would a woman's tottering bark be tossed
Where stoutest ships, the men of wit, are lost?
When I reflect on this, I straight grow wise,
And my own self thus gravely I advise:
--Dear Artemesia, poetry's a snare;
Bedlam has many mansions; have a care.
Your muse diverts you, makes the reader sad:
Consider, too, 'twill be discreetly done
To make yourself the fiddle of the town,
To find th' ill-humored pleasure at their need,
Cursed if you fail, and scorned though you succeed!
Thus, like an errant woman as I am,
No sooner well convinced writing's a shame,
That whore is scarce a more reproachful name
Than poetess-

7

John Wilmot, the Earl of Rochester

Like men that marry, or like maids that woo,
'Cause 'tis the very worst thing they can do,
Pleased with the contradiction and the sin,
Methinks I stand n thorns till I begin.
--Y' expect at least to hear what loves have passed
In this lewd town, since you and I met last;
What change has happened of intrigues, and whether
The old ones last, and who and who's together.
But how, my dearest Chloe, shall I set
My pet to write what I would fain forget?
Or name that lost thing, love, without a tear,
Since so debauched by ill-bred customs here?
Love, the most generous passion of the mind,
The softest refuge innocence can find,
The safe director of unguided youth,
Fraught with kind wishes, and secured by truth;
That cordial drop heaven in our cup has thrown
To make the nauseous draught of life go down;
On which one only blessing; God might raise
In lands of atheists, subsidies of praise,
For none did e'er so dull and stupid prove
But felt a god, and blessed his power in love -
This only joy for which poor we were made
Is grown, like play, to be an arrant trade.
The rooks creep in, and it has got of late
As many little cheats and tricks as that.
--But what yet more a woman's heart would vex,
'Tis chiefly carried on by our own sex;
Our silly sex! who, born like monarchs free,
turn gypsies for a meaner liberty,
And hate restraint, though but from infamy.
They call whatever is not common, nice,
And deaf to nature's rule, or love's advice,

Forsake the pleasure to pursue the vice.
To an exact perfection they have wrought
The action, love; the passion is forgot.
'Tis below wit, they tell you, to admire,
And ev'n without approving, they desire.
Their private wish obeys the public vice;
'Twixt good and bad, whimsey decides, not choice.
Fashions grow up for taste; at forms they strike;
They know what they would have, not what they like.
Bovey's a beauty, of some few agree
To call him so; the rest to that degree
Affected are, that with their ears they see.
--Where I was visiting the other night
Comes a fine lady, with her humble knight,
Who had prevailed on her, through her own skill,
At his request, thought much against his will,
To come to London.
As the coach stopped, we heard her voice, more loud
Than a great-bellied woman's in a crowd,
Telling the knight that her affairs require
He, for some hours, obsequiously retire.
I think she was ashamed to have him seen:
Hard fate of husbands! The gallant had been,
Though a diseased, ill-favored fool, brought in.
"Dispatch," says she, "that business you pretend,
Your beastly visit to your drunken friend!
A bottle ever makes you look so fine;
Methinks I long to smell you stink of wine!
Your country drinking breath's enough to kill:
Sour ale corrected with a lemon peel.
Prithee, farewell! We'll meet again anon."
The necessary thing bows, and is gone.
--She flies upstairs, and all the haste does show

9

That fifty antic postures will allow,
And then bursts out: "Dear madam, am not I
The altered'st creature breathing? Let me die,
I find myself ridiculously grown,
Embarassee with being out of town,
Rude and untaught like any Indian queen:
My country nakedness is strangely seen.
--"How is love governed, love that rules the state,
And pray, who are the men most worn of late?
When I was married, fools were a la mode.
The men of wit were then held incommode,
Slow of belief, and fickle in desire,
Who, ere they'll be persuaded, must inquire
As if they came to spy, not to admire.
With searching wisdom, fatal to their ease,
They still find out why what may, should not please;
Nay, take themselves for injured when we dare
Make 'em think better of us than we are,
And if we hide our frailties from their sights,
Call us deceitful jilts and hypocrites.
They little guess, who at our arts are grieved,
The perfect joy of being well deceived;
Inquisitive as jealous cuckolds grow:
Rather than not be knowing, they will know
What, being known, creates their certain woe.
Women should these, of all mankind avoid,
For wonder by clear knowledge is destroyed.
Woman, who is an arrant bird of knight,
Bold in the dusk before a fool's dull sight,
Should fly when reason brings the glaring light.
--"But the kind, easy fool, apt to admire
Himself, trusts us; his follies all conspire
To flatter his, and favor our desire.

Vain of his proper merit, he with ease
Believes we love him best who best can please.
On him our gross, dull, common flatteries pass,
Ever most joyful when most made an ass.
Heavy to apprehend, though all mankind
Perceive us false, the fop concerned is blind,
Who, doting on himself,
Thinks everyone that sees him of his mind.
These are true women's men."

------------------------- Here forced to cease
Through want of breath, not will to hold her peace,
She to the window runs, where she had spied
Her much esteemed dear friend, the monkey, tied.
With forty smiles, as many antic bows,
As if 't had been the lady of the house,
The dirty, chattering monster she embraced,
And made it this fine, tender speech at last:
"Kiss me, thou curious miniature of man!
How odd thou art! how pretty! how japan!
Oh, I could live and die with thee!" Then on
For half an hour in compliment she run.
--I took this time to think what nature meant
When this mixed thing into the world she sent,
So very wise, yet so impertinent:
One who knew everything; who, God thought fit,
Should be an ass through choice, not want of wit;
Whose foppery, without the help of sense,
Could ne'er have rose to such an excellence.
Nature's as lame in making a true fop
As a philosopher; the very top
And dignity of folly we attain
By studious search, and labor of the brain,

11

By observation, counsel, and deep thought:
God never made a coxcomb worth a groat.
We owe that name to industry and arts:
An eminent fool must be a fool of parts.
And such a one was she, who had turned o'er
As many books as men; loved much, read more;
Had a discerning wit; to her was known
Everyone's fault and merit, but her own.
All the good qualities that ever blessed
A woman so distinguished from the rest,
Except discretion only, she possessed.
--But now, "Mon cher dear Pug," she cries, "adieu!"
And the discourse broke off does thus renew:
--"You smile to see me, whom the world perchance
Mistakes to have some wit, so far advance
The interest of fools, that I approve
Their merit, more than men's of wit, in love.
But, in our sex, too many proofs there are
Of such whom wits undo, and fools repair.
This, in my time, was so observed a rule
Hardly a wench in town but had her fool.
The meanest common slut, who long was grown
The jest and scorn of every pit buffoon,
Had yet left charms enough to have subdued
Some fop or other, fond to be thought lewd.
Foster could make an Irish lord a Nokes,
And Betty Morris had her City cokes.
A woman's ne'er so ruined but she can
Be still revenged on her undoer, man;
How lost so'er, she'll find some lover, more
A lewd, abandoned fool than she a whore.
--"That wretched thing Corinna, who had run
Through all the several ways of being undone,

Cozened at first by love, and living then
By turning the too dear-bought trick on men -
Gay were the hours, and winged with joys they flew,
When first the town her early beauties knew;
Courted, admired, and loved, with presents fed;
Youth in her looks, and pleasure in her bed;
Till fate, or her ill angel, thought it fit
To make her dote upon a man of wit,
Who found 'twas dull to love above a day;
Made his ill-natured jest, and went away.
Now scorned by all, forsaken, and oppressed,
She's a momento mori to the rest;
Diseased, decayed, to take up half a crown
Must mortgage her long scarf and manteau gown.
Poor creature! who, unheard of as a fly,
In some dark hole must all the winter lie,
And want and dirt endure a while half year
That for one month she tawdry may appear.
--"In Easter Term she gets her a new gown,
When my young master's worship comes to town,
From pedagogue and mother just set free,
The heir and hopes of a great family;
Which, with strong ale and beef, the country rules,
And ever since the Conquest have been fools.
And now, with careful prospect to maintain
The character, lest crossing of the strain
Should mend the booby breed, his friends provide
A cousin of his own to be his bride.
And thus set out
With an estate, no wit, and a young wife
(The solid comforts of a coxcomb's life),
Dunghill and pease forsook, he comes to town,
Turns spark, learns to be lewd, and is undone.

Nothing suits worse with vice than want of sense:
Fools are still wicked at their own expense.
--"This o'ergrown schoolboy lost Corinna wins,
And at first dash to make an ass begins:
Pretends to like a man who has not known
The vanities nor vices of the town;
Fresh in his youth, and faithful in his love;
Eager of joys which he does seldom prove;
Healthful and strong, he does no pains endure
But what the fair one he adores can cure;
Grateful for favors, does the sex esteem,
And libels none for being kind to him;
Then of the lewdness of the times complains:
Rails at the wits and atheists, and maintains
'Tis better than good sense, than power or wealth,
To have a love untainted, youth, and health.
--"The unbred puppy, who had never seen
A creature look so gay, or talk so fine,
Believes, then falls in love, and then in debt;
Mortgages all, ev'n to the ancient seat,
To buy this mistress a new house for life;
To give her plate and jewels, robs his wife.
And when t' th' height of fondness he is grown,
'Tis time to poison him, and all's her own.
Thus meeting in her common arms his fate,
He leaves her bastard heir to his estate,
And, as the race of such an owl deserves,
His own dull lawful progeny he starves.
--"Nature, who never made a thing in vain,
But does each insect to some end ordain,
Wisely contrived kind keeping fools, no doubt,
To patch up vices men of wit wear out."
Thus she ran on two hours, some grains of sense

Still mixed with volleys of impertinence.
--But now 'tis time I should some pity show
To Chloe, since I cannot choose but know
Readers must reap the dullness writers sow.
But the next post such stories I will tell
As, joined with these, shall to a volumn swell,
As true as heaven, more infamous than hell.
But you are tired, and so am I.
Farewell.

John Wilmot

John Wilmot, the Earl of Rochester

A Ramble in St. James's Park

Much wine had passed, with grave discourse
Of who fucks who, and who does worse
(Such as you usually do hear
From those that diet at the Bear),
When I, who still take care to see
Drunkenness relieved by lechery,
Went out into St. James's Park
To cool my head and fire my heart.
But though St. James has th' honor on 't,
'Tis consecrate to prick and cunt.
There, by a most incestuous birth,
Strange woods spring from the teeming earth;
For they relate how heretofore,
When ancient Pict began to whore,
Deluded of his assignation
(Jilting, it seems, was then in fashion),
Poor pensive lover, in this place
Would frig upon his mother's face;
Whence rows of mandrakes tall did rise
Whose lewd tops fucked the very skies.
Each imitative branch does twine
In some loved fold of Aretine,
And nightly now beneath their shade
Are buggeries, rapes, and incests made.
Unto this all-sin-sheltering grove
Whores of the bulk and the alcove,
Great ladies, chambermaids, and drudges,
The ragpicker, and heiress trudges.

John Wilmot, the Earl of Rochester

Carmen, divines, great lords, and tailors,
Prentices, poets, pimps, and jailers,
Footmen, fine fops do here arrive,
And here promiscuously they swive.

Along these hallowed walks it was
That I beheld Corinna pass.
Whoever had been by to see
The proud disdain she cast on me
Through charming eyes, he would have swore
She dropped from heaven that very hour,
Forsaking the divine abode
In scorn of some despairing god.
But mark what creatures women are:
How infinitely vile, when fair!

Three knights o' the' elbow and the slur
With wriggling tails made up to her.

The first was of your Whitehall baldes,
Near kin t' th' Mother of the Maids;
Graced by whose favor he was able
To bring a friend t' th' Waiters' table,
Where he had heard Sir Edward Sutton
Say how the King loved Banstead mutton;
Since when he'd ne'er be brought to eat
By 's good will any other meat.
In this, as well as all the rest,
He ventures to do like the best,
But wanting common sense, th' ingredient
In choosing well not least expedient,
Converts abortive imitation
To universal affectation.

Thus he not only eats and talks
But feels and smells, sits down and walks,
Nay looks, and lives, and loves by rote,
In an old tawdry birthday coat.

The second was a Grays Inn wit,
A great inhabiter of the pit,
Where critic-like he sits and squints,
Steals pocket handkerchiefs, and hints
From 's neighbor, and the comedy,
To court, and pay, his landlady.

The third, a lady's eldest son
Within few years of twenty-one
Who hopes from his propitious fate,
Against he comes to his estate,
By these two worthies to be made
A most accomplished tearing blade.

One, in a strain 'twixt tune and nonsense,
Cries, "Madam, I have loved you long since.
Permit me your fair hand to kiss";
When at her mouth her cunt cries, "Yes!"
In short, without much more ado,
Joyful and pleased, away she flew,
And with these three confounded asses
From park to hackney coach she passes.

So a proud bitch does lead about
Of humble curs the amorous rout,
Who most obsequiously do hunt
The savory scent of salt-swoln cunt.
Some power more patient now relate

John Wilmot, the Earl of Rochester

The sense of this surprising fate.
Gods! that a thing admired by me
Should fall to so much infamy.
Had she picked out, to rub her arse on,
Some stiff-pricked clown or well-hung parson,
Each job of whose spermatic sluice
Had filled her cunt with wholesome juice,
I the proceeding should have praised
In hope sh' had quenched a fire I raised.
Such natural freedoms are but just:
There's something generous in mere lust.
But to turn a damned abandoned jade
When neither head nor tail persuade;
To be a whore in understanding,
A passive pot for fools to spend in!
The devil played booty, sure, with thee
To bring a blot on infamy.

But why am I, of all mankind,
To so severe a fate designed?
Ungrateful! Why this treachery
To humble fond, believing me,
Who gave you privilege above
The nice allowances of love?
Did ever I refuse to bear
The meanest part your lust could spare?
When your lewd cunt came spewing home
Drenched with the seed of half the town,
My dram of sperm was supped up after
For the digestive surfeit water.
Full gorged at another time
With a vast meal of slime
Which your devouring cunt had drawn

From porters' backs and footmen's brawn,
I was content to serve you up
My ballock-full for your grace cup,
Nor ever thought it an abuse
While you had pleasure for excuse -
You that could make my heart away
For noise and color, and betray
The secrets of my tender hours
To such knight-errant paramours,
When, leaning on your faithless breast,
Wrapped in security and rest,
Soft kindness all my powers did move,
And reason lay dissolved in love!

May stinking vapors choke your womb
Such as the men you dote upon
May your depraved appetite,
That could in whiffling fools delight,
Beget such frenzies in your mind
You may go mad for the north wind,
And fixing all your hopes upon't
To have him bluster in your cunt,
Turn up your longing arse t' th' air
And perish in a wild despair!
But cowards shall forget to rant,
Schoolboys to frig, old whores to paint;
The Jesuits' fraternity
Shall leave the use of buggery;
Crab-louse, inspired with grace divine,
From earthly cod to heaven shall climb;
Physicians shall believe in Jesus,
And disobedience cease to please us,
Ere I desist with all my power

To plague this woman and undo her.
But my revenge will best be timed
When she is married that is limed.
In that most lamentable state
I'll make her feel my scorn and hate:
Pelt her with scandals, truth or lies,
And her poor cur with jealousied,
Till I have torn him from her breech,
While she whines like a dog-drawn bitch;
Loathed and despised, kicked out o' th' Town
Into some dirty hole alone,
To chew the cud of misery
And know she owes it all to me.

And may no woman better thrive
That dares prophane the cunt I swive!

A Satyre Against Mankind

Were I - who to my cost already am
One of those strange, prodigious creatures, man -
A spirit free to choose for my own share
What sort of flesh and blood I pleased to wear,
I'd be a dog, a monkey, or a bear,
Or anything but that vain animal,
Who is so proud of being rational.

— big, bulky, glaring, flagrant faults & vices

His senses are too gross; and he'll contrive
reason A sixth, to contradict the other five;
And before certain instinct will prefer
Reason, which fifty times for one does err.
Reason, an ignis fatuus of the mind, *— will o the wisp –*
Which leaving light of nature, sense, behind, *light above marshes*
Pathless and dangerous wand'ring ways it takes, *as approached*
Through Error's fenny bogs and thorny brakes; *appears to recede*
Whilst the misguided follower climbs with pain
Mountains of whimsey's, heaped in his own brain;
Stumbling from thought to thought, falls headlong down,
Into Doubt's boundless sea where, like to drown,
Books bear him up awhile, and make him try
To swim with bladders of Philosophy;
In hopes still to o'ertake the escaping light;
The vapour dances, in his dancing sight,
Till spent, it leaves him to eternal night.
Then old age and experience, hand in hand,
Lead him to death, make him to understand,
After a search so painful, and so long,

John Wilmot, the Earl of Rochester

That all his life he has been in the wrong:

Huddled In dirt the reasoning engine lies,
Who was so proud, so witty, and so wise.
Pride drew him in, as cheats their bubbles catch,
And made him venture; to be made a wretch.
His wisdom did has happiness destroy,
Aiming to know that world he should enjoy;
And Wit was his vain, frivolous pretence
Of pleasing others, at his own expense.
For wits are treated just like common whores,
First they're enjoyed, and then kicked out of doors;
The pleasure past, a threatening doubt remains,
That frights th' enjoyer with succeeding pains:
Women and men of wit are dangerous tools,
And ever fatal to admiring fools.
Pleasure allures, and when the fops escape,
'Tis not that they're beloved, but fortunate,
And therefore what they fear, at heart they hate:

But now, methinks some formal band and beard
Takes me to task; come on sir, I'm prepared:

"Then by your Favour, anything that's writ
Against this jibing, jingling knack called Wit
Likes me abundantly: but you take care
Upon this point not to be too severe.
Perhaps my Muse were fitter for this part,
For I profess I can be very smart
On Wit, which I abhor with all my heart;
I long to lash it in some sharp essay,
But your grand indiscretion bids me stay,
And turns my tide of ink another way.

What rage Torments in your degenerate mind,
To make you rail at reason, and mankind
Blessed glorious man! To whom alone kind heaven
An everlasting soul hath freely given;
Whom his great maker took such care to make,
That from himself he did the image take;
And this fair frame in shining reason dressed,
To dignify his nature above beast.
Reason, by whose aspiring influence
We take a flight beyond material sense,
Dive into mysteries, then soaring pierce
The flaming limits of the universe,
Search heaven and hell, Find out what's acted there,
And give the world true grounds of hope and fear."

Hold mighty man, I cry, all this we know,
From the pathetic pen of Ingelo;
From Patrlck's Pilgrim, Sibbes' Soliloquies,
And 'tis this very reason I despise,
This supernatural gift that makes a mite
Think he's an image of the infinite;
Comparing his short life, void of all rest,
To the eternal, and the ever-blessed.
This busy, pushing stirrer-up of doubt,
That frames deep mysteries, then finds them out;
Filling with frantic crowds of thinking fools
The reverend bedlam's, colleges and schools;
Borne on whose wings each heavy sot can pierce
The limits of the boundless universe;
So charming ointments make an old witch fly,
And bear a crippled carcass through the sky.
'Tis the exalted power whose business lies
In nonsense and impossibilities.

Saying Superstition and reason have the same aims

This made a whimsical philosopher
Before the spacious world his tub prefer,
And we have modern cloistered coxcombs, who
Retire to think 'cause they have nought to do.
But thoughts are given for action's government;
Where action ceases, thought's impertinent:
Our sphere of action is life's happiness,
And he that thinks beyond thinks like an ass.

Thus, whilst against false reasoning I inveigh.
I own right reason, which I would obey:
That reason which distinguishes by sense,
And gives us rules of good and ill from thence;
That bounds desires. with a reforming will
To keep 'em more in vigour, not to kill. -
Your reason hinders, mine helps to enjoy,
Renewing appetites yours would destroy.
My reason is my friend, yours is a cheat,
Hunger calls out, my reason bids me eat;
Perversely. yours your appetite does mock:
This asks for food, that answers, 'what's o'clock'
This plain distinction, sir, your doubt secures,
'Tis not true reason I despise, but yours.
Thus I think reason righted, but for man,
I'll ne'er recant, defend him if you can:
For all his pride, and his philosophy,
'Tis evident: beasts are in their own degree
As wise at least, and better far than he.

Those creatures are the wisest who attain. -
By surest means. the ends at which they aim.
If therefore Jowler finds and kills the hares,
Better than Meres supplies committee chairs;

Though one's a statesman, th' other but a hound,
Jowler in justice would be wiser found.
You see how far man's wisdom here extends.
Look next if human nature makes amends;
Whose principles are most generous and just,
- And to whose morals you would sooner trust:

Be judge yourself, I'll bring it to the test,
Which is the basest creature, man or beast
Birds feed on birds, beasts on each other prey,
But savage man alone does man betray:
Pressed by necessity; they kill for food,
Man undoes man, to do himself no good.
With teeth and claws, by nature armed, they hunt
Nature's allowance, to supply their want.
But man, with smiles, embraces. friendships. Praise,
Inhumanely his fellow's life betrays;
With voluntary pains works his distress,
Not through necessity, but wantonness.
For hunger or for love they bite, or tear,
Whilst wretched man is still in arms for fear.
For fear he arms, and is of arms afraid:
From fear, to fear, successively betrayed.
Base fear, the source whence his best passions came.
His boasted honour, and his dear-bought fame.
The lust of power, to whom he's such a slave,
And for the which alone he dares be brave;
To which his various projects are designed,
Which makes him generous, affable, and kind.
For which he takes such pains to be thought wise,
And screws his actions, in a forced disguise;
Leads a most tedious life in misery,
Under laborious, mean hypocrisy.

Look to the bottom of his vast design,
Wherein man's wisdom, power, and glory join:
The good he acts. the ill he does endure.
'Tis all from fear, to make himself secure.
Merely for safety after fame they thirst,
For all men would be cowards if they durst.
And honesty's against all common sense,
Men must be knaves, 'tis in their own defence.
Mankind's dishonest: if you think it fair
Among known cheats to play upon the square,
You'll be undone.
Nor can weak truth your reputation save,
The knaves will all agree to call you knave.
Wronged shall he live, insulted o'er, oppressed,
Who dares be less a villain than the rest.

Thus sir, you see what human nature craves,
Most men are cowards, all men should be knaves;
The difference lies, as far as I can see.
Not in the thing itself, but the degree;
And all the subject matter of debate
Is only, who's a knave of the first rate

All this with indignation have I hurled
At the pretending part of the proud world,
Who, swollen with selfish vanity, devise,
False freedoms, holy cheats, and formal lies,
Over their fellow slaves to tyrannise.

But if in Court so just a man there be,
(In Court, a just man - yet unknown to me)
Who does his needful flattery direct
Not to oppress and ruin, but protect:

Since flattery, which way soever laid,
Is still a tax: on that unhappy trade.
If so upright a statesman you can find,
Whose passions bend to his unbiased mind,
Who does his arts and policies apply
To raise his country, not his family;
Nor while his pride owned avarice withstands,
Receives close bribes, from friends corrupted hands.

Is there a churchman who on God relies
Whose life, his faith and doctrine justifies
Not one blown up, with vain prelatic pride,
Who for reproofs of sins does man deride;
Whose envious heart makes preaching a pretence
With his obstreperous, saucy eloquence,
To chide at kings, and rail at men of sense;
Who from his pulpit vents more peevlsh lies,
More bitter railings, scandals, calumnies,
Than at a gossiping are thrown about
When the good wives get drunk, and then fall out.
None of that sensual tribe, whose talents lie
In avarice, pride, sloth, and gluttony.
Who hunt good livings; but abhor good lives,
Whose lust exalted, to that height arrives,
They act adultery with their own wives.
And ere a score of years completed be,
Can from the loftiest pulpit proudly see,
Half a large parish their own progeny.
Nor doting bishop, who would be adored
For domineering at the Council board;

A greater fop, in business at fourscore,
Fonder of serious toys, affected more,

29

Than the gay, glittering fool at twenty proves,
With all his noise, his tawdry clothes and loves.
But a meek, humble man, of honest sense,
Who preaching peace does practise continence;
Whose pious life's a proof he does believe
Mysterious truths which no man can conceive.

If upon Earth there dwell such god-like men,
I'll here recant my paradox to them,
Adores those shrines of virtue, homage pay,
And with the rabble world their laws obey.

If such there are, yet grant me this at least,
Man differs more from man than man from beast.

A Satyre on Charles II

[Rochester had to flee the court for several months after
handing this to the King by mistake.]

In th' isle of Britain, long since famous grown
For breeding the best cunts in Christendom,
There reigns, and oh! long may he reign and thrive,
The easiest King and best bred man alive.
Him no ambition moves to get reknown
Like the French fool, that wanders up and down
Starving his people, hazarding his crown.
Peace is his aim, his gentleness is such,
And love he loves, for he loves fucking much.
Nor are his high desires above his strength:
His scepter and his prick are of a length;
And she may sway the one who plays with th' other,
And make him little wiser than his brother.
Poor Prince! thy prick, like thy buffoons at court,
Will govern thee because it makes thee sport.
'Tis sure the sauciest prick that e'er did swive,
The proudest, peremptoriest prick alive.
Though safety, law, religion, life lay on 't,
'Twould break through all to make its way to cunt.
Restless he rolls about from whore to whore,
A merry monarch, scandalous and poor.
To Carwell, the most dear of all his dears,
The best relief of his declining years,
Oft he bewails his fortune, and her fate:

To love so well, and be beloved so late.
Yet his dull, graceless bollocks hang an arse.
This you'd believe, had I but time to tell ye
The pains it costs to poor, laborious Nelly,
Whilst she employs hands, fingers, mouth, and thighs,
Ere she can raise the member she enjoys.
All monarchs I hate, and the thrones they sit on,
From the hector of France to the cully of Britain.

A Song of a Young Lady to Her Ancient Lover

Ancient Person, for whom I
All the flattering youth defy,
Long be it e'er thou grow old,
Aching, shaking, crazy cold;
But still continue as thou art,
Ancient Person of my heart.

On thy withered lips and dry,
Which like barren furrows lie,
Brooding kisses I will pour,
Shall thy youthful heart restore,
Such kind show'rs in autumn fall,
And a second spring recall;
Nor from thee will ever part,
Ancient Person of my heart.

Thy nobler parts, which but to name
In our sex would be counted shame,
By ages frozen grasp possest,
From their ice shall be released,
And, soothed by my reviving hand,
In former warmth and vigour stand.
All a lover's wish can reach,
For thy joy my love shall teach;
And for thy pleasure shall improve
All that art can add to love.

John Wilmot, the Earl of Rochester

Yet still I love thee without art,
Ancient Person of my heart.

A Woman's Honour

Love bade me hope, and I obeyed;
Phyllis continued still unkind:
Then you may e'en despair, he said,
In vain I strive to change her mind.

Honour's got in, and keeps her heart,
Durst he but venture once abroad,
In my own right I'd take your part,
And show myself the mightier God.

This huffing Honour domineers
In breasts alone where he has place:
But if true generous Love appears,
The hector dares not show his face.

Let me still languish and complain,
Be most unhumanly denied:
I have some pleasure in my pain,
She can have none with all her pride.

I fall a sacrifice to Love,
She lives a wretch for Honour's sake;
Whose tyrant does most cruel prove,
The difference is not hard to make.

Consider real Honour then,
You'll find hers cannot be the same;

John Wilmot, the Earl of Rochester

'Tis noble confidence in men,
In women, mean, mistrustful shame.

Absent of Thee I Languish Still

Absent from thee I languish still;
Then ask me not, when I return?
The straying fool 'twill plainly kill
To wish all day, all night to mourn.

Dear! from thine arms then let me fly,
That my fantastic mind may prove
The torments it deserves to try
That tears my fixed heart from my love.

When, wearied with a world of woe,
To thy safe bosom I retire
where love and peace and truth does flow,
May I contented there expire,

Lest, once more wandering from that heaven,
I fall on some base heart unblest,
Faithless to thee, false, unforgiven,
And lose my everlasting rest.

John Wilmot, the Earl of Rochester

All My Past Life...

All my past life is mine no more,
The flying hours are gone,
Like transitory dreams given o'er,
Whose images are kept in store
By memory alone.

What ever is to come is not,
How can it then be mine?
The present moment's all my lot,
And that as fast as it is got,
Phyllis, is wholly thine.

Then talk not of inconstancy,
False hearts, and broken vows,
Ii, by miracle, can be,
This live-long minute true to thee,
'Tis all that heaven allows.

John Wilmot, the Earl of Rochester

An Allusion to Horace

Well Sir, 'tis granted, I said Dryden's Rhimes,
Were stoln, unequal, nay dull many times:
What foolish Patron, is there found of his,
So blindly partial, to deny me this?
But that his Plays, Embroider'd up and downe,
With Witt, and Learning, justly pleas'd the Towne,
In the same paper, I as freely owne:
Yet haveing this allow'd, the heavy Masse,
That stuffs up his loose Volumes must not passe:
For by that Rule, I might as well admit,
Crownes tedious Scenes, for Poetry, and Witt.
'Tis therefore not enough, when your false Sense
Hits the false Judgment of an Audience
Of Clapping-Fooles, assembling a vast Crowd
'Till the throng'd Play-House, crack with the dull Load;
Tho' ev'n that Tallent, merits in some sort,
That can divert the Rabble and the Court:
Which blundring Settle, never cou'd attaine,
And puzling Otway, labours at in vaine.
But within due proportions, circumscribe
What e're you write; that with a flowing Tyde,
The Stile, may rise, yet in its rise forbeare,
With uselesse Words, t'oppresse the wearyed Eare:
Here be your Language lofty, there more light,
Your Rethorick, with your Poetry, unite:
For Elegance sake, sometimes alay the force

Of Epethets; 'twill soften the discourse;
A Jeast in Scorne, poynts out, and hits the thing,
More home, than the Morosest Satyrs Sting.
Shakespeare, and Johnson, did herein excell,
And might in this be Immitated well;
Whom refin'd Etheridge, Coppys not at all,
But is himself a Sheere Originall:
Nor that Slow Drudge, in swift Pindarique straines,
Flatman, who Cowley imitates with paines,
And rides a Jaded Muse, whipt with loose Raines.
When Lee, makes temp'rate Scipio, fret and Rave,
And Haniball, a whineing Am'rous Slave;
I laugh, and wish the hot-brain'd Fustian Foole,
In Busbys hands, to be well lasht at Schoole.
Of all our Moderne Witts, none seemes to me,
Once to have toucht upon true Comedy,
But hasty Shadwell, and slow Witcherley.
Shadwells unfinisht workes doe yet impart,
Great proofes of force of Nature, none of Art.
With just bold Stroakes, he dashes here and there,
Shewing great Mastery with little care;
And scornes to varnish his good touches o're,
To make the Fooles, and Women, praise 'em more.
But Witcherley, earnes hard, what e're he gaines,
He wants noe Judgment, nor he spares noe paines;
He frequently excells, and at the least,
Makes fewer faults, than any of the best.
Waller, by Nature for the Bayes design'd,
With force, and fire, and fancy unconfin'd,
In Panigericks does Excell Mankind:
He best can turne, enforce, and soften things,
To praise great Conqu'rours, or to flatter Kings.
For poynted Satyrs, I wou'd Buckhurst choose,

The best good Man, with the worst Natur'd Muse:
For Songs, and Verses, Mannerly Obscene,
That can stirr Nature up, by Springs unseene,
And without forceing blushes, warme the Queene:
Sidley, has that prevailing gentle Art,
That can with a resistlesse Charme impart,
The loosest wishes to the Chastest Heart,
Raise such a Conflict, kindle such a ffire
Betwixt declineing Virtue, and desire,
Till the poor Vanquisht Maid, dissolves away,
In Dreames all Night, in Sighs, and Teares, all Day.
Dryden, in vaine, try'd this nice way of Witt,
For he, to be a tearing Blade thought fit,
But when he wou'd be sharp, he still was blunt,
To friske his frollique fancy, hed cry Cunt;
Wou'd give the Ladyes, a dry Bawdy bob,
And thus he got the name of Poet Squab:
But to be just, twill to his praise be found,
His Excellencies, more than faults abound.
Nor dare I from his Sacred Temples teare,
That Lawrell, which he best deserves to weare.
But does not Dryden find ev'n Johnson dull?
Fletcher, and Beaumont, uncorrect, and full
Of Lewd lines as he calls em? Shakespeares Stile
Stiffe, and Affected? To his owne the while
Allowing all the justnesse that his Pride,
Soe Arrogantly, had to these denyd?
And may not I, have leave Impartially
To search, and Censure, Drydens workes, and try,
If those grosse faults, his Choyce Pen does Commit
Proceed from want of Judgment, or of Witt.
Of if his lumpish fancy does refuse,
Spirit, and grace to his loose slatterne Muse?

Five Hundred Verses, ev'ry Morning writ,
Proves you noe more a Poet, than a Witt.
Such scribling Authors, have beene seene before,
Mustapha, the English Princesse, Forty more,
Were things perhaps compos'd in Half an Houre.
To write what may securely stand the test
Of being well read over Thrice oat least
Compare each Phrase, examin ev'ry Line,
Weigh ev'ry word, and ev'ry thought refine;
Scorne all Applause the Vile Rout can bestow,
And be content to please those few, who know.
Canst thou be such a vaine mistaken thing
To wish thy Workes might make a Play-house ring,
With the unthinking Laughter, and poor praise
Of Fopps, and Ladys, factious for thy Plays?
Then send a cunning Friend to learne thy doome,
From the shrew'd Judges in the Drawing-Roome.
I've noe Ambition on that idle score,
But say with Betty Morice, heretofore
When a Court-Lady, call'd her Buckleys Whore,
I please one Man of Witt, am proud on't too,
Let all the Coxcombs, dance to bed to you.
Shou'd I be troubled when the Purblind Knight
Who squints more in his Judgment, than his sight,
Picks silly faults, and Censures what I write?
Or when the poor-fed Poets of the Towne
For Scrapps, and Coach roome cry my Verses downe?
I loath the Rabble, 'tis enough for me,
If Sidley, Shadwell, Shepherd, Witcherley,
Godolphin, Buttler, Buckhurst, Buckingham,
And some few more, whom I omit to name
Approve my Sense, I count their Censure Fame.

By All Love's Soft, Yet Mighty Powers

By all love's soft, yet mighty powers,
It is a thing unfit,
That men should fuck in time of flowers,
Or when the smock's beshit.

Fair nasty nymph, be clean and kind,
And all my joys restore;
By using paper still behind,
And sponges for before.

My spotless flames can ne'er decay,
If after every close,
My smoking prick escape the fray,
Without a bloody nose.

If thou would have me true, be wise,
And take to cleanly sinning,
None but fresh lovers' pricks can rise,
At Phyllis in foul linen.

John Wilmot, the Earl of Rochester

Constancy

I cannot change, as others do,
Though you unjustly scorn;
Since that poor swain, that sighs for you
For you alone was born.
No, Phyllis, no, your heart to move
A surer way I'll try:
And to revenge my slighted love,
Will still love on, will still love on, and die.

When, kill'd with grief, Amyntas lies;
And you to mind shall call
The sighs that now unpitied rise;
The tears that vainly fall:
That welcome hour that ends this smart,
Will then begin your pain;
For such a faithful, tender heart
Can never break, can never break in vain.

John Wilmot, the Earl of Rochester

Epitaph on Charles II

Here lies a great and mighty King,
Whose promise none relied on;
He never said a foolish thing,
Nor ever did a wise one.

John Wilmot, the Earl of Rochester

Give Me Leave to Rail at You

Give me leave to rail at you, -
I ask nothing but my due:
To call you false, and then to say
You shall not keep my heart a day.
But alas! against my will
I must be your captive still.
Ah! be kinder, then, for I
Cannot change, and would not die.

Kindness has resistless charms;
All besides but weakly move;
Fiercest anger it disarms,
And clips the wings of flying love.
Beauty does the heart invade,
Kindness only can persuade;
It gilds the lover's servile chain,
And makes the slave grow pleased again.

John Wilmot, the Earl of Rochester

I Cannot Change, As Others Do

I cannot change, as others do,
Though you unjustly scorn;
Since that poor swain that sighs for you,
For you alone was born.
No, Phyllis, no, your heart to move
A surer way I'll try:
And to revenge my slighted love,
Will still love on, will still love on, and die.

When, killed with grief, Amintas lies
And you to mind shall call,
The sighs that now unpitied rise,
The tears that vainly fall,
That welcome hour that ends this smart
Will then begin your pain;
For such a faithful tender heart
Can never break, can never break in vain.

John Wilmot, the Earl of Rochester

Love and Life

All my past life is mine no more,
The flying hours are gone,
Like transitory dreams giv'n o'er,
Whose images are kept in store
By memory alone.

The time that is to come is not;
How can it then be mine?
The present moment's all my lot;
And that, as fast as it is got,
Phyllis, is only thine.

Then talk not of inconstancy,
False hearts, and broken vows;
If I, by miracle, can be
This live-long minute true to thee,
'Tis all that Heav'n allows.

John Wilmot, the Earl of Rochester

My Dear Mistress Has a Heart

My dear mistress has a heart
Soft as those kind looks she gave me,
When with love's resistless art,
And her eyes, she did enslave me;
But her constancy's so weak,
She's so wild and apt to wander,
That my jealous heart would break
Should we live one day asunder.

Melting joys about her move,
Killing pleasures, wounding blisses;
She can dress her eyes in love,
And her lips can arm with kisses;
Angels listen when she speaks,
She's my delight, all mankind's wonder;
But my jealous heart would break
Should we live one day asunder.

John Wilmot, the Earl of Rochester

Poems to Mulgrave and Scroope

Deare Friend.

I heare this Towne does soe abound,
With sawcy Censurers, that faults are found,
With what of late wee (in Poetique Rage)
Bestowing, threw away on the dull Age;
But (howsoe're Envy, their Spleen may raise,
To Robb my Brow, of the deserved Bays)
Their thanks at least I merit since through me,
They are Partakers of your Poetry;
And this is all, I'll say in my defence,
T'obtaine one Line, of your well worded Sense

I'd be content t'have writ the Brittish Prince.
I'm none of those who thinke themselves inspir'd,
Nor write with the vaine hopes to be admir'd;
But from a Rule (I have upon long tryall)
T'avoyd with care, all sort of self denyall.
Which way soe're desire and fancy leade
(Contemning Fame) that Path I boldly tread;
And if exposeing what I take for Witt,
To my deare self, a Pleasure I beget,
Noe matter tho' the Censring Crittique fret.
Those whom my Muse displeases, are at strife
With equall Spleene, against my Course of life,
The least delight of which, I'd not forgoe,

For all the flatt'ring Praise, Man can bestow.
If I designd to please the way were then,
To mend my Manners, rather than my Pen;
The first's unnaturall, therefore unfit,
And for the Second, I despair of it,
Since Grace, is not soe hard to get as Witt.
Perhaps ill Verses, ought to be confin'd,
In meere good Breeding, like unsav'ry Wind;
Were Reading forc'd, I shou'd be apt to thinke
Men might noe more write scurvily, than stinke:
But 'tis your choyce, whether you'll Read, or noe,
If likewise of your smelling it were soe,
I'd Fart just as I write, for my owne ease,
Nor shou'd you be concern'd, unlesse you please:
I'll owne, that you write better than I doe,
But I have as much need to write, as you.
What though the Excrement of my dull Braine,

Runns in a harsh, insipid Straine,
Whilst your rich Head, eases it self of Witt?
Must none but Civet-Catts, have leave to shit?
In all I write, shou'd Sense, and Witt, and Rhyme
Faile me at once, yet something soe Sublime,
Shall stamp my Poem, that the World may see,
It cou'd have beene produc'd, by none but me.
And that's my end, for Man, can wish noe more,
Then soe to write, as none ere writ before.
Yet why am I noe Poet, of the tymes?
I have Allusions, Similies and Rhymes,
And Witt, or else 'tis hard that I alone,
Of the whole Race of Mankind, shou'd have none.
Unequally, the Partiall Hand of Heav'n,
Has all but this one only Blessing giv'n;

The World appeares like a great Family,
Whose Lord opprest with Pride, and Poverty,
(That to a few, great Plenty he may show)
Is faine to starve the Num'rous Traine below:
Just soe seemes Providence, as poor and vaine,
Keeping more Creatures, than it can maintaine.
Here 'tis profuse, and there it meanly saves,
And for One Prince, it makes Ten Thousand Slaves:
In Witt alone, it has beene Magnificent,
Of which, soe just a share, to each is sent
That the most Avaricious are content.
For none e're thought, (the due Division's such),
His owne too little, or his Friends too much.
Yet most Men shew, or find great want of Witt,
Writeing themselves, or Judging what is writ:
But I, who am of sprightly Vigour full
Looke on Mankind, as Envious, and dull.
Borne to my self, my self I like alone,
And must conclude my Judgment good, or none.
(For shou'd my Sense be nought, how cou'd I know,
Whether another Man's, were good, or noe?)
Thus, I resolve of my owne Poetry,
That 'tis the best, and there's a Fame for me.
If then I'm happy, what does it advance,
Whether to merit due, or Arrogance?

Oh! but the World will take offence thereby,
Why then the World, shall suffer for't, not I.
Did e're this sawcy World, and I agree?
To let it have its Beastly will on me?
Why shou'd my Prostituted Sense, be drawne,
To ev'ry Rule, their musty Customes spawne?
But Men, will Censure you; Tis Two to one

When e're they Censure, they'll be in the wrong.
There's not a thing on Earth, that I can name
Soe foolish, and soe false, as Common Fame.
It calls the Courtier Knave, the plaine Man rude,
Haughty the grave, and the delightfull Lewd.
Impertinent the briske, Morosse the sad,
Meane the Familiar, the Reserv'd one Mad.
Poor helplesse Woman, is not favour'd more
She's a slye Hipocryte, or Publique Whore.
Then who the Devill, wou'd give this -- to be free
From th'Innocent Reproach of Infamy?
These things consider'd, make me (in despight
Of idle Rumour,) keepe at home, and write.

John Wilmot

Portsmouth's Looking Glass

Methinks I see you, newly risen
From your embroider'd Bed and pissing,
With studied mien and much grimace,
Present yourself before your glass,
To vanish and smooth o'er those graces,
You rubb'd off in your Night Embraces.

John Wilmot, the Earl of Rochester

Satyr

Were I (who to my cost already am
One of those strange prodigious Creatures Man)
A Spirit free, to choose for my own share,
What Case of Flesh, and Blood, I pleas'd to weare,
I'd be a Dog, a Monkey, or a Bear,
Or any thing but that vain Animal,
Who is so proud of being rational.
The senses are too gross, and he'll contrive
A Sixth, to contradict the other Five;
And before certain instinct, will preferr
Reason, which Fifty times for one does err.
Reason, an Ignis fatuus, in the Mind,
Which leaving light of Nature, sense behind;
Pathless and dang'rous wandring ways it takes,
Through errors Fenny -- Boggs, and Thorny Brakes;
Whilst the misguided follower, climbs with pain,
Mountains of Whimseys, heap'd in his own Brain:
Stumbling from thought to thought, falls headlong down,
Into doubts boundless Sea, where like to drown,
Books bear him up awhile, and make him try,
To swim with Bladders of Philosophy;
In hopes still t'oretake th'escaping light,
The Vapour dances in his dazling sight,
Till spent, it leaves him to eternal Night.
Then Old Age, and experience, hand in hand,
Lead him to death, and make him understand,

After a search so painful, and so long,
That all his Life he has been in the wrong;
Hudled in dirt, the reas'ning Engine lyes,
Who was so proud, so witty, and so wise.
Pride drew him in, as Cheats, their Bubbles catch,
And makes him venture, to be made a Wretch.
His wisdom did his happiness destroy,
Aiming to know that World he shou'd enjoy;
And Wit, was his vain frivolous pretence,
Of pleasing others, at his own expence.
For Witts are treated just like common Whores,
First they're enjoy'd, and then kickt out of Doores:
The pleasure past, a threatning doubt remains,
That frights th'enjoyer, with succeeding pains:
Women and Men of Wit, are dang'rous Tools,
And ever fatal to admiring Fools.
Pleasure allures, and when the Fopps escape,
'Tis not that they're belov'd, but fortunate,
And therefore what they fear, at heart they hate.
But now methinks some formal Band, and Beard,
Takes me to task, come on Sir I'm prepar'd.
Then by your favour, any thing that's writ
Against this gibeing jingling knack call'd Wit,
Likes me abundantly, but you take care,
Upon this point, not to be too severe.
Perhaps my Muse, were fitter for this part,
For I profess, I can be very smart
On Wit, which I abhor with all my heart:
I long to lash it in some sharp Essay,
But your grand indiscretion bids me stay,
And turns my Tide of Ink another way.
What rage ferments in your degen'rate mind,
To make you rail at Reason, and Mankind?

Blest glorious Man! to whom alone kind Heav'n,
An everlasting Soul has freely giv'n;
Whom his great Maker took such care to make,
That from himself he did the Image take;
And this fair frame, in shining Reason drest,
To dignifie his Nature, above Beast.
Reason, by whose aspiring influence,
We take a flight beyond material sense,
Dive into Mysteries, then soaring pierce,
The flaming limits of the Universe,
Search Heav'n and Hell, find out what's acted there,
And give the World true grounds of hope and fear.
Hold mighty Man, I cry, all this we know,
From the Pathetique Pen of Ingello;
From Patricks Pilgrim, Stilling fleets replyes,
And 'tis this very reason I despise.
This supernatural gift, that makes a Myte -- ,
Think he's the Image of the Infinite:
Comparing his short life, void of all rest,
To the Eternal, and the ever blest.
This busie, puzling, stirrer up of doubt,
That frames deep Mysteries, then finds 'em out;
Filling with Frantick Crowds of thinking Fools,
Those Reverend Bedlams, Colledges, and Schools;
Borne on whose Wings, each heavy Sot can pierce,
The limits of the boundless Universe.
So charming Oyntments, make an Old Witch flie,
And bear a Crippled Carcass through the Skie.
'Tis this exalted Pow'r, whose bus'ness lies,
In Nonsense, and impossibilities.
This made a Whimsical Philosopher,
Before the spacious World, his Tub prefer,
And we have modern Cloysterd Coxcombs, who

Retire to think, cause they have naught to do.
But thoughts, are giv'n, for Actions government,
Where Action ceases, thoughts impertinent:
Our Sphere of Action, is lifes happiness,
And he who thinks Beyond, thinks like an Ass.
Thus, whilst against false reas'ning I inveigh,
I own right Reason, which I wou'd obey:
That Reason that distinguishes by sense,
And gives us Rules, of good, and ill from thence:
That bounds desires, with a reforming Will,
To keep 'em more in vigour, not to kill.
Your Reason hinders, mine helps t'enjoy,
Renewing Appetites, yours wou'd destroy.
My Reason is my Friend, yours is a Cheat,
Hunger call's out, my Reason bids me eat;
Perversly yours, your Appetite does mock,
This asks for Food, that answers what's a Clock?
This plain distinction Sir your doubt secures,
'Tis not true Reason I despise but yours.
Thus I think Reason righted, but for Man,
I'le nere recant defend him if you can.
For all his Pride, and his Philosophy,
'Tis evident, Beasts are in their degree,
As wise at least, and better far than he.
Those Creatures, are the wisest who attain,
By surest means, the ends at which they aim.
If therefore Jowler, finds, and Kills his Hares,
Better than Meres, supplyes Committee Chairs;
Though one's a States-man, th'other but a Hound,
Jowler, in Justice, wou'd be wiser found.
You see how far Mans wisedom here extends,
Look next, if humane Nature makes amends;
Whose Principles, most gen'rous are, and just,

And to whose Moralls, you wou'd sooner trust.
Be judge your self, I'le bring it to the test,
Which is the basest Creature Man, or Beast?
Birds, feed on Birds, Beasts, on each other prey,
But Savage Man alone, does Man, betray:
Prest by necessity, they Kill for Food,
Man, undoes Man, to do himself no good.
With Teeth, and Claws, by Nature arm'd they hunt,
Natures allowance, to supply their want.
But Man, with smiles, embraces, Friendships, praise,
Unhumanely his Fellows life betrays;
With voluntary pains, works his distress,
Not through necessity, but wantonness.
For hunger, or for Love, they fight, or tear,
Whilst wretched Man, is still in Arms for fear;
For fear he armes, and is of Armes afraid,
By fear, to fear, successively betray'd.
Base fear, the source whence his best passion came,
His boasted Honor, and his dear bought Fame.
That lust of Pow'r, to which he's such a Slave,
And for the which alone he dares be brave:
To which his various Projects are design'd,
Which makes him gen'rous, affable, and kind.
For which he takes such pains to be thought wise,
And screws his actions, in a forc'd disguise:
Leading a tedious life in Misery,
Under laborious, mean Hypocrisie.
Look to the bottom, of his vast design,
Wherein Mans Wisdom, Pow'r, and Glory joyn;
The good he acts, the ill he does endure,
'Tis all for fear, to make himself secure.
Meerly for safety, after Fame we thirst,
For all Men, wou'd be Cowards if they durst.

And honesty's against all common sense,
Men must be Knaves, 'tis in their own defence.
Mankind's dishonest, if you think it fair,
Amongst known Cheats, to play upon the square,
You'le be undone --
Nor can weak truth, your reputation save,
The Knaves, will all agree to call you Knave.
Wrong'd shall he live, insulted o're, opprest,
Who dares be less a Villain, than the rest.
Thus Sir you see what humane Nature craves,
Most Men are Cowards, all Men shou'd be Knaves:
The diff'rence lyes (as far as I can see)
Not in the thing it self, but the degree;
And all the subject matter of debate,
Is only who's a Knave, of the first Rate?
All this with indignation have I hurl'd,
At the pretending part of the proud World,
Who swolne with selfish vanity, devise,
False freedomes, holy Cheats, and formal Lyes
Over their fellow Slaves to tyrannize.
But if in Court, so just a Man there be,
(In Court, a just Man, yet unknown to me)
Who does his needful flattery direct,
Not to oppress, and ruine, but protect;
Since flattery, which way so ever laid,
Is still a Tax on that unhappy Trade.
If so upright a States-Man, you can find,
Whose passions bend to his unbyass'd Mind;
Who does his Arts, and Pollicies apply,
To raise his Country, not his Family;
Nor while his Pride own'd Avarice withstands,
Receives close Bribes, from Friends corrupted hands.
Is there a Church-Man who on God relyes?

Whose Life, his Faith, and Doctrine Justifies?
Not one blown up, with vain Prelatique Pride,
Who for reproof of Sins, does Man deride:
Whose envious heart makes preaching a pretence
With his obstrep'rous sawcy Eloquence,
To chide at Kings, and raile at Men of sense.
Who from his Pulpit, vents more peevish Lyes,
More bitter railings, scandals, Calumnies,
Than at a Gossipping, are thrown about,
When the good Wives, get drunk, and then fall out.
None of that sensual Tribe, whose Tallents lye,
In Avarice, Pride, Sloth, and Gluttony.
Who hunt good Livings, but abhor good Lives,
Whose Lust exalted, to that height arrives,
They act Adultery with their own Wives.
And e're a score of Years compleated be,
Can from the lofty Pulpit proudly see,
Half a large Parish, their own Progeny.
Nor doating Bishop who wou'd be ador'd,
For domineering at the Councel Board;
A greater Fop, in business at Fourscore,
Fonder of serious Toyes, affected more,
Than the gay glitt'ring Fool, at Twenty proves,
With all his noise, his tawdrey Cloths, and Loves.
But a meek humble Man, of honest sense,
Who Preaching peace, does practice continence;
Whose pious life's a proof he does believe,
Misterious truths, which no Man can conceive.
If upon Earth there dwell such God-like Men,
I'le here recant my Paradox to them,
Adore those Shrines of Virtue, Homage pay,
And with the Rabble World, their Laws obey.
If such there are, yet grant me this at least,

John Wilmot, the Earl of Rochester

Man differs more from Man, than Man from Beast.

Signior Dildo

You ladies of merry England
Who have been to kiss the Duchess's hand,
Pray, did you not lately observe in the show
A noble Italian called Signior Dildo?

This signior was one of the Duchess's train
And helped to conduct her over the main;
But now she cries out, 'To the Duke I will go,
I have no more need for Signior Dildo.'

At the Sign of the Cross in St James's Street,
When next you go thither to make yourselves sweet
By buying of powder, gloves, essence, or so,
You may chance to get a sight of Signior Dildo.

You would take him at first for no person of note,
Because he appears in a plain leather coat,
But when you his virtuous abilities know,
You'll fall down and worship Signior Dildo.

My Lady Southesk, heaven prosper her for't,
First clothed him in satin, then brought him to court;
But his head in the circle he scarcely durst show,
So modest a youth was Signior Dildo.

The good Lady Suffolk, thinking no harm,

Had got this poor stranger hid under her arm.
Lady Betty by chance came the secret to know
And from her own mother stole Signior Dildo.

The Countess of Falmouth, of whom people tell
Her footmen wear shirts of a guinea an ell,
Might save that expense, if she did but know
How lusty a swinger is Signior Dildo.

By the help of this gallant the Countess of Rafe
Against the fierce Harris preserved herself safe;
She stifled him almost beneath her pillow,
So closely she embraced Signior Dildo.

The pattern of virtue, Her Grace of Cleveland,
Has swallowed more pricks than the ocean has sand;
But by rubbing and scrubbing so wide does it grow,
It is fit for just nothing but Signior Dildo.

Our dainty fine duchesses have got a trick
To dote on a fool for the sake of his prick,
The fops were undone did their graces but know
The discretion and vigour of Signior Dildo.

The Duchess of Modena, though she looks so high,
With such a gallant is content to lie,
And for fear that the English her secrets should know,
For her gentleman usher took Signior Dildo.

The Countess o'th'Cockpit (who knows not her name?
She's famous in story for a killing dame),
When all her old lovers forsake her, I trow,
She'll then be contented with Signior Dildo.

Red Howard, red Sheldon, and Temple so tall
Complain of his absence so long from Whitehall.
Signior Barnard has promised a journey to go
And bring back his countryman, Signior Dildo.

Doll Howard no longer with His Highness must range,
And therefore is preferred this civil exchange:
Her teeth being rotten, she smells best below,
And needs must be fitted for Signior Dildo.

St Albans with wrinkles and smiles in his face,
Whose kindness to strangers becomes his high place,
In his coach and six horses is gone to Bergo
To take the fresh air with Signior Dildo.

Were this signior but known to the citizen fops,
He'd keep their fine wives from the foremen o'their shops;
But the rascals deserve their horns should still grow
For burning the Pope and his nephew, Dildo.

Tom Killigrew's wife, that Holland fine flower,
At the sight of this signior did fart and belch sour,
And her Dutch breeding the further to show,
Says, 'Welcome to England, Mynheer Van Dildo.'

He civilly came to the Cockpit one night,
And proferred his service to fair Madam Knight.
Quoth she, 'I intrigue with Captain Cazzo;
Your nose in mine arse, good Signior Dildo.'

This signior is sound, safe, ready, and dumb
As ever was candle, carrot, or thumb;

Then away with these nasty devices, and show
How you rate the just merit of Signior Dildo.

Count Cazzo, who carries his nose very high,
In passion he swore his rival should die;
Then shut himself up to let the world know
Flesh and blood could not bear it from Signior Dildo.

A rabble of pricks who were welcome before,
Now finding the porter denied them the door,
Maliciously waited his coming below
And inhumanly fell on Signior Dildo.

Nigh wearied out, the poor stranger did fly,
And along the Pall Mall they followed full cry;
The women concerned from every window
Cried, 'For heaven's sake, save Signior Dildo.'

The good Lady Sandys burst into a laughter
To see how the ballocks came wobbling after,
And had not their weight retarded the foe,
Indeed't had gone hard with Signior Dildo.

Song

Quoth the Duchess of Cleveland to counselor Knight,
"I'd fain have a prick, knew I how to come by't.
I desire you'll be secret and give your advice:
Though cunt be not coy, reputation is nice."

"To some cellar in Sodom Your Grace must retire
Where porters with black-pots sit round a coal fire;
There open your case, and Your Grace cannot fail
Of a dozen of pricks for a dozen of ale."

"Is't so?" quoth the Duchess. "Aye, by God!" quoth the whore.
"Then give me the key that unlocks the back door,
For I'd rather be fucked by porters and carmen
Than thus be abused by Churchill and Jermyn."

John Wilmot, the Earl of Rochester

The Disabled Debauchee

As some brave admiral, in former war,
Deprived of force, but pressed with courage still,
Two rival fleets appearing from afar,
Crawls to the top of an adjacent hill;

From whence (with thoughts full of concern) he views
The wise and daring conduct of the fight,
And each bold action to his mind renews
His present glory, and his past delight;

From his fierce eyes, flashes of rage he throws,
As from black clouds when lightning breaks away,
Transported, thinks himself amidst his foes,
And absent yet enjoys the bloody day;

So when my days of impotence approach,
And I'm by pox and wine's unlucky chance,
Driven from the pleasing billows of debauch,
On the dull shore of lazy temperance,

My pains at last some respite shall afford,
Whilst I behold the battles you maintain,
When fleets of glasses sail about the board,
From whose broadsides volleys of wit shall rain.

Nor shall the sight of honourable scars,

John Wilmot, the Earl of Rochester

Which my too-forward valour did procure,
Frighten new-listed soldiers from the wars.
Past joys have more than paid what I endure.

Should hopeful youths (worth being drunk) prove nice,
And from their fair inviters meanly shrink,
'Twould please the ghost of my departed vice,
If at my counsel they repent and drink.

Or should some cold-complexioned set forbid,
With his dull morals, our night's brisk alarms,
I'll fire his blood by telling what I did,
When I was strong and able to bear arms.

I'll tell of whores attacked, their lords at home,
Bawds' quarters beaten up, and fortress won,
Windows demolished, watches overcome,
And handsome ills by my contrivance done.

Nor shall our love-fits, Cloris, be forgot,
When each the well-looked link-boy strove t'enjoy,
And the best kiss was the deciding lot:
Whether the boy fucked you, or I the boy.

With tales like these I will such heat inspire,
As to important mischief shall incline.
I'll make them long some ancient church to fire,
And fear no lewdness they're called to by wine.

Thus statesman-like, I'll saucily impose,
And safe from danger valiantly advise,
Sheltered in impotence, urge you to blows,
And being good for nothing else, be wise.

The Imperfect Enjoyment

Naked she lay, clasped in my longing arms,
I filled with love, and she all over charms;
Both equally inspired with eager fire,
Melting through kindness, flaming in desire.
With arms,legs,lips close clinging to embrace,
She clips me to her breast, and sucks me to her face.
Her nimble tongue, Love's lesser lightening, played
Within my mouth, and to my thoughts conveyed
Swift orders that I should prepare to throw
The all-dissolving thunderbolt below.
My fluttering soul, sprung with the painted kiss,
Hangs hovering o'er her balmy brinks of bliss.
But whilst her busy hand would guide that part
Which should convey my soul up to her heart,
In liquid raptures I dissolve all o'er,
Melt into sperm and, and spend at every pore.
A touch from any part of her had done't:
Her hand, her foot, her very look's a cunt.

Smiling, she chides in a kind murmuring noise,
And from her body wipes the clammy joys,
When, with a thousand kisses wandering o'er
My panting bosom, "Is there then no more?"
She cries. "All this to love and rapture's due;
Must we not pay a debt to pleasure too?"

But I, the most forlorn, lost man alive,
To show my wished obedience vainly strive:
I sigh, alas! and kiss, but cannot swive.
Eager desires confound my first intent,
Succeeding shame does more success prevent,
And rage at last confirms me impotent.
Ev'n her fair hand, which might bid heat return
To frozen age, and make cold hermits burn,
Applied to my dead cinder, warms no more
Than fire to ashes could past flames restore.
Trembling, confused, despairing, limber, dry,
A wishing, weak, unmoving lump I lie.
This dart of love, whose piercing point, oft tried,
With virgin blood ten thousand maids have dyed;
Which nature still directed with such art
That it through every cunt reached every heart -
Stiffly resolved, 'twould carelessly invade
Woman or man, nor aught its fury stayed:
Where'er it pierced, a cunt it found or made -
Now languid lies in this unhappy hour,
Shrunk up and sapless like a withered flower.

Thou treacherous, base deserter of my flame,
False to my passion, fatal to my fame,
Through what mistaken magic dost thou prove
So true to lewdness, so untrue to love?
What oyster-cinder-beggar-common whore
Didst thou e'er fail in all thy life before?
When vice, disease, and scandal lead the way,
With what officious haste dost thou obey!
Like a rude, roaring hector in the streets
Who scuffles, cuffs, and justles all he meets,
But if his king or country claim his aid,

The rakehell villain shrinks and hides his head;
Ev'n so thy brutal valour is displayed,
Breaks every stew, does each small whore invade,
But when great Love the onset does command,
Base recreant to thy prince, thou dar'st not stand.
Worst part of me, and henceforth hated most,
Through all the town a common fucking-post,
On whom each whore relieves her tingling cunt
As hogs do rub themselves on gates and grunt,
May'st thou to ravenous chancres be a prey,
Or in consuming weepings waste away;
May strangury and stone thy days attend;
May'st thou ne'er piss, who did refuse to spend
When all my joys did on false thee depend.
And may ten thousand abler pricks agree
To do the wronged Corinna right for thee.

John Wilmot, the Earl of Rochester

The Mistress

An age in her embraces passed
Would seem a winter's day;
When life and light, with envious haste,
Are torn and snatched away.

But, oh! how slowly minutes roll.
When absent from her eyes
That feed my love, which is my soul,
It languishes and dies.

For then no more a soul but shade
It mournfully does move
And haunts my breast, by absence made
The living tomb of love.

You wiser men despise me not,
Whose love-sick fancy raves
On shades of souls and Heaven knows what;
Short ages live in graves.

Whene'er those wounding eyes, so full
Of sweetness, you did see,
Had you not been profoundly dull,
You had gone mad like me.

Nor censure us, you who perceive

John Wilmot, the Earl of Rochester

My best beloved and me
Sign and lament, complain and grieve;
You think we disagree.

Alas, 'tis sacred jealousy,
Love raised to an extreme;
The only proof 'twixt her and me,
We love, and do not dream.

Fantastic fancies fondly move
And in frail joys believe,
Taking false pleasure for true love;
But pain can ne'er deceive.

Kind jealous doubts, tormenting fears,
And anxious cares when past,
Prove our heart's treasure fixed and dear,
And make us blessed at last.

The Platonic Lady

I could love thee till I die,
Would'st thou love me modestly,
And ne'er press, whilst I live,
For more than willingly I would give:
Which should sufficient be to prove
I'd understand the art of love.

I hate the thing is called enjoyment:
Besides it is a dull employment,
It cuts off all that's life and fire
From that which may be termed desire;
Just like the bee whose sting is gone
Converts the owner to a drone.

I love a youth will give me leave
His body in my arms to wreathe;
To press him gently, and to kiss;
To sigh, and look with eyes that wish
For what, if I could once obtain,
I would neglect with flat disdain.

I'd give him liberty to toy
And play with me, and count it joy.
Our freedom should be full complete,
And nothing wanting but the feat.
Let's practice, then, and we shall prove

John Wilmot, the Earl of Rochester

These are the only sweets of love.

To His Mistress

Why dost thou shade thy lovely face? O why
Does that eclipsing hand of thine deny
The sunshine of the Sun's enlivening eye?

Without thy light what light remains in me?
Thou art my life; my way, my light's in thee;
I live, I move, and by thy beams I see.

Thou art my life-if thou but turn away
My life's a thousand deaths. Thou art my way-
Without.thee, Love, I travel not but stray.

My light thou art-without thy glorious sight
My eyes are darken'd with eternal night.
My Love, thou art my way, my life, my light.

Thou art my way; I wander if thou fly.
Thou art my light; if hid, how blind am I!
Thou art my life; if thou withdraw'st, I die.

My eyes are dark and blind, I cannot see:
To whom or whither should my darkness flee,
But to that light?-and who's that light but thee?

If I have lost my path, dear lover, say,
Shall I still wander in a doubtful way?

John Wilmot, the Earl of Rochester

Love, shall a lamb of Israel's sheepfold stray?

My path is lost, my wandering steps do stray;
I cannot go, nor can I safely stay;
Whom should I seek but thee, my path, my way?

And yet thou turn'st thy face away and fly'st me!
And yet I sue for grace and thou deny'st me!
Speak, art thou angry, Love, or only try'st me?

Thou art the pilgrim's path, the blind man's eye,
The dead man's life. On thee my hopes rely:
If I but them remove, I surely die.

Dissolve thy sunbeams, close thy wings and stay!
See, see how I am blind, and dead, and stray!
-O thou art my life, my light, my way!

Then work thy will! If passion bid me flee,
My reason shall obey, my wings shall be
Stretch'd out no farther than from me to thee!

To This Moment a Rebel

To this moment a rebel I throw down my arms,
Great Love, at first sight of Olinda's bright charms.
Make proud and secure by such forces as these,
You may now play the tyrant as soon as you please.

When Innocence, Beauty, and Wit do conspire
To betray, and engage, and inflame my Desire,
Why should I decline what I cannot avoid?
And let pleasing Hope by base Fear be destroyed?

Her innocence cannot contrive to undo me,
Her beauty's inclined, or why should it pursue me?
And Wit has to Pleasure been ever a friend,
Then what room for Despair, since Delight is Love's end?

There can be no danger in sweetness and youth,
Where Love is secured by good nature and truth;
On her beauty I'll gaze and of pleasure complain
While every kind look adds a link to my chain.

'Tis more to maintain than it was to surprise,
But her Wit leads in triumpth the slave of her eyes;
I beheld, with the loss of my freedom before,
But hearing, forever must serve and adore.

Too bright is my Goddess, her temple too weak:

John Wilmot, the Earl of Rochester

Retire, divine image! I feel my heart break.
Help, Love! I dissolve in a rapture of charms
At the thought of those joys I should meet in her arms.

Tunbridge Wells

At five this morn, when Phoebus raised his head
From Thetis' lap, I raised myself from bed,
And mounting steed, I trotted to the waters
The rendesvous of fools, buffoons, and praters,
Cuckolds, whores, citizens, their wives and daughters.

My squeamish stomach I with wine had bribed
To undertake the dose that was prescribed;
But turning head, a sudden cursèd view
That innocent provision overthrew,
And without drinking, made me purge and spew.
From coach and six a thing unweildy rolled,
Whose lumber, card more decently would hold.
As wise as calf it looked, as big as bully,
But handled, proves a mere Sir Nicholas Cully;
A bawling fop, a natural Nokes, and yet
He dares to censure as if he had wit.
To make him more ridiculous, in spite
Nature contrived the fool should be a knight.
Though he alone were dismal signet enough,
His train contributed to set him off,
All of his shape, all of the selfsame stuff.
No spleen or malice need on them be thrown:
Nature has done the business of lampoon,
And in their looks their characters has shown.

Endeavoring this irksome sight to balk,
And a more irksome noise, their silly talk,
I silently slunk down t' th' Lower Walk,
But often when one would Charybdis shun,
Down upon Scilla 'tis one's fate to run,
For here it was my curséd luck to find
As great a fop, though of another kind,
A tall stiff fool that walked in Spanish guise:
The buckram puppet never stirred its eyes,
But grave as owl it looked, as woodcock wise.
He scorns the empty talking of this mad age,
And speaks all proverbs, sentences, and adage;
Can with as much solemnity buy eggs
As a cabal can talk of their intrigues;
Master o' th' Ceremonies, yet can dispense
With the formality of talking sense.

From hence unto the upper walk I ran,
Where a new scene of foppery began.
A tribe of curates, priests, canonical elves,
Fit company for none besides themselves,
Were got together. Each his distemper told,
Scurvy, stone, strangury; some were so bold
To charge the spleen to be their misery,
And on that wise disease brought infamy.
But none had modesty enough t' complain
Their want of learning, honesty, and brain,
The general diseases of that train.
These call themselves ambassadors of heaven,
And saucily pretend commissions given;
But should an Indian king, whose small command
Seldom extends beyond ten miles of land,
Send forth such wretched tools in an ambassage,

He'd find but small effects of such a message.
Listening, I found the cob of all this rabble
Pert Bays, with his importance comfortable.
He, being raised to an archdeaconry
By trampling on religion, liberty,
Was grown to great, and looked too fat and jolly,
To be disturbed with care and melancholy,
Though Marvell has enough exposed his folly.
He drank to carry off some old remains
His lazy dull distemper left in 's veins.
Let him drink on, but 'tis not a whole flood
Can give sufficient sweetness to his blood
To make his nature of his manners good.

Next after these, a fulsome Irish crew
Of silly Macs were offered to my view.
The things did talk, but th' hearing what they said
I did myself the kindness to evade.
Nature has placed these wretches beneath scorn:
They can't be called so vile as they are born.
Amidst the crowd next I myself conveyed,
For now were come, whitewash and paint being laid,
Mother and daughter, mistress and the maid,
And squire with wig and pantaloon displayed.
But ne'er could conventicle, play, or fair
For a true medley, with this herd compare.
Here lords, knights, squires, ladies and countesses,
Chandlers, mum-bacon women, sempstresses
Were mixed together, nor did they agree
More in their humors than their quality.

Here waiting for gallant, young damsel stood,
Leaning on cane, and muffled up in hood.

The would-be wit, whose business was to woo,
With hat removed and solemn scrape of shoe
Advanceth bowing, then genteelly shrugs,
And ruffled foretop into order tugs,
And thus accosts her: "Madam, methinks the weather
Is grown much more serene since you came hither.
You influence the heavens; but should the sun
Withdraw himself to see his rays outdone
By your bright eyes, they would supply the morn,
And make a day before the day be born."
With mouth screwed up, conceited winking eyes,
And breasts thrust forward, "Lord, sir!" she replies.
"It is your goodness, and not my deserts,
Which makes you show this learning, wit, and parts."
He, puzzled, butes his nail, both to display
The sparkling ring, and think what next to say,
And thus breaks forth afresh: "Madam, egad!
Your luck at cards last night was very bad:
At cribbage fifty-nine, and the next show
To make the game, and yet to want those two.
God damn me, madam, I'm the son of a whore
If in my life I saw the like before!"
To peddler's stall he drags her, and her breast
With hearts and such-like foolish toys he dressed;
And then, more smartly to expound the riddle
Of all his prattle, gives her a Scotch fiddle.

Tired with this dismal stuff, away I ran
Where were two wives, with girl just fit for man -
Short-breathed, with pallid lips and visage wan.
Some curtsies past, and the old compliment
Of being glad to see each other, spent,
With hand in hand they lovingly did walk,

And one began thus to renew the talk:
"I pray, good madam, if it may be thought
No rudeness, what cause was it hither brought
Your ladyship?" She soon replying, smiled,
"We have a good estate, but have no child,
And I'm informed these wells will make a barren
Woman as fruitful as a cony warren."
The first returned, "For this cause I am come,
For I can have no quietness at home.
My husband grumbles though we have got one,
This poor young girl, and mutters for a son.
And this is grieved with headache, pangs, and throes;
Is full sixteen, and never yet had those."
She soon replied, "Get her a husband, madam:
I married at that age, and ne'er had 'em;
Was just like her. Steel waters let alone:
A back of steel will bring 'em better down."
And ten to one but they themselves will try
The same means to increase their family.
Poor foolish fribble, who by subtlety
Of midwife, truest friend to lechery,
Persuaded art to be at pains and charge
To give thy wife occasion to enlarge
Thy silly head! For here walk Cuff and Kick,
With brawny back and legs and potent prick,
Who more substantially will cure thy wife,
And on her half-dead womb bestow new life.
From these the waters got the reputation
Of good assistants unto generation.

Some warlike men were now got into th' throng,
With hair tied back, singing a bawdy song.
Not much afraid, I got a nearer view,

And 'twas my chance to know the dreadful crew.
They were cadets, that seldom can appear:
Damned to the stint of thirty pounds a year.
With hawk on fist, or greyhound led in hand,
The dogs and footboys sometimes they command.
But now, having trimmed a cast-off spavined horse,
With three hard-pinched-for guineas in their purse,
Two rusty pistols, scarf about the arse,
Coat lined with red, they here presume to swell:
This goes for captain, that for colonel.
So the Bear Garden ape, on his steed mounted,
No longer is a jackanapes accounted,
But is, by virtue of his trumpery, then
Called by the name of "the young gentleman."

Bless me! thought I, what thing is man, that thus
In all his shapes, he is ridiculous?
Ourselves with noise of reason we do please
In vain: humanity's our worst disease.
Thrice happy beasts are, who, because they be
Of reason void, and so of foppery.
Faith, I was so ashamed that with remorse
I used the insolence to mount my horse;
For he, doing only things fit for his nature,
Did seem to me by much the wiser creature.

Upon His Drinking a Bowl

Vulcan, contrive me such a cup
As Nestor used of old;
Show all thy skill to trim it up,
Damask it round with gold.

Make it so large that, filled with sack
Up to the swelling brim,
Vast toasts on the delicious lake
Like ships at sea may swim.

Engrave not battle on its cheek:
With war I've nought to do;
I'm none of those that took Maastricht,
Nor Yarmouth leaguer knew.

Let it no name of planets tell,
Fixed stars, or constellations;
For I am no Sir Sidrophel,
Nor none of his relations.

But carve theron a spreading vine,
Then add two lovely boys;
Their limbs in amorous folds intwine,
The type of future joys.

Cupid and Bacchus my saints are,

John Wilmot, the Earl of Rochester

May drink and love still reign,
With wine I wash away my cares,
And then to cunt again.

Upon Nothing

Nothing, thou elder brother even to shade,
That hadst a being ere the world was made,
And (well fixed) art alone of ending not afraid.
Ere time and place were, time and place were not,
When primitive Nothing Something straight begot,
Then all proceeded from the great united--What?
Something, the general attribute of all,
Severed from thee, its sole original,
Into thy boundless self must undistinguished fall.
Yet Something did thy mighty power command,
And from thy fruitful emptiness's hand,
Snatched men, beasts, birds, fire, air, and land.
Matter, the wickedest offspring of thy race,
By Form assisted, flew from thy embrace,
And rebel Light obscured thy reverend dusky face.
With Form and Matter, Time and Place did join,
Body, thy foe, with these did leagues combine
To spoil thy peaceful realm, and ruin all thy line.
But turncoat Time assists the foe in vain,
And, bribed by thee, assists thy short-lived reign,
And to thy hungry womb drives back thy slaves again.
Though mysteries are barred from laic eyes,
And the Divine alone with warrant pries
Into thy bosom, where thy truth in private lies,
Yet this of thee the wise may freely say,
Thou from the virtuous nothing takest away,

And to be part of thee the wicked wisely pray.
Great Negative, how vainly would the wise
Inquire, define, distinguish, teach, devise?
Didst thou not stand to point their dull philosophies.
Is, or is not, the two great ends of Fate,
And true or false, the subject of debate,
That perfects, or destroys, the vast designs of Fate,
When they have racked the politician's breast,
Within thy bosom most securely rest,
And, when reduced to thee, are least unsafe and best.
But Nothing, why does Something still permit
That sacred monarchs should at council sit
With persons highly thought at best for nothing fit?
Whist weighty Something modestly abstains
From princes' coffers, and from statesmen's brains,
And Nothing there like stately Nothing reigns,
Nothing, who dwellest with fools in grave disguise,
For whom they reverend shapes and forms devise,
Lawn sleeves, and furs, and gowns, when they like thee look
wise.
French truth, Dutch prowess, British policy,
Hibernian learning, Scotch civility,
Spaniard's dispatch, Dane's wit are mainly seen in thee.
The great man's gratitude to his best friend,
King's promises, whore's vows, towards thee they bend,
Flow swiftly to thee, and in thee never end.

Printed in the United States
64768LVS00007B/202-240